A   F i r e s i d e   B o o k

P u b l i s h e d   b y   S i m o n   &   S c h u s t e r

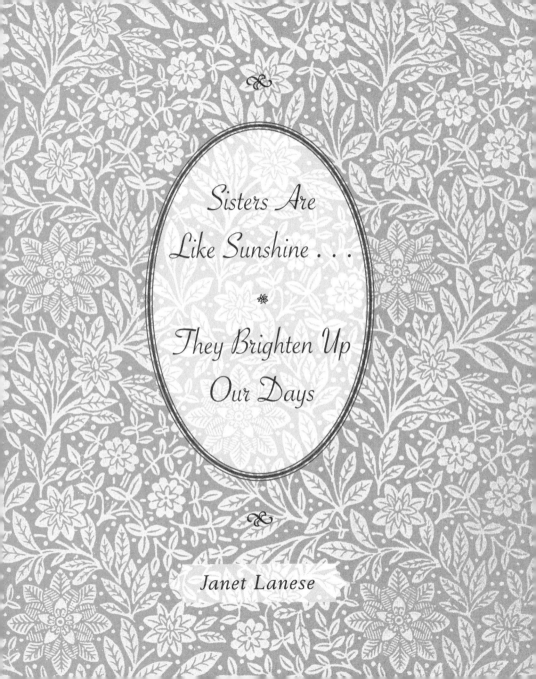

Sisters Are Like Sunshine . . .

They Brighten Up Our Days

Janet Lanese

FIRESIDE
Rockefeller Center
1230 Avenue of the Americas
New York, NY 10020

FIRESIDE and colophon are registered trademarks of Simon & Schuster Inc.
Permissions Acknowledgments appear on page 109.

Designed by Judy Wong

Manufactured in the United States of America

3   5   7   9   10   8   6   4   2

Library of Congress Cataloging-in-Publication Data:
Lanese, Janet.
Sisters are like sunshine : they brighten up our days / Janet Lanese.
p.   cm.
"Fireside book"—P. 2
1. Sisters—Quotations, maxims, etc.   I. Title.
PN6084.S56L36   1998
306.875—dc21   98-34134
CIP
ISBN 0-684-84252-1

Acknowledgments

Thanks again to the winning team in the editorial
department at Fireside Books: Trish Todd, Betsy
Radin Herman, and Matthew Walker.
And bravo to Laurie Harper, the marketing genius
at Sebastian Agency.

To Bettye Flynn, Elloise Miller, and Glenna Adams,
three Texas Bluebonnets whose lifelong sister
act has upstaged the Gabors'

Contents

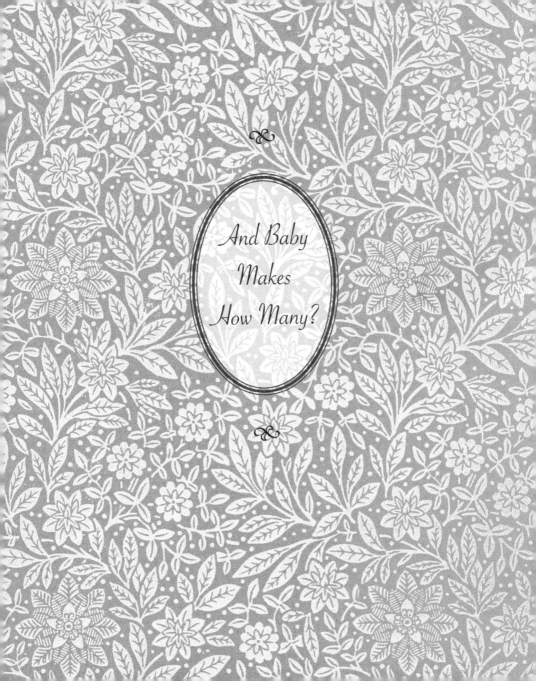

And Baby
Makes
How Many?

SOME THINGS DON'T MAKE ANY SENSE AT ALL

My mom says I'm her sugarplum,
My mom says I'm her lamb.
My mom says I'm completely perfect
Just the way I am.
My mom says I'm a super-special
Wonderful, terrific, little guy.
My mom just had another baby.
Why?

Judith Viorst

It didn't take me long to figure out that the new baby was here for
a long visit. After all, she'd taken off all her clothes.

Susie, age seven

Mother: "Aren't you thrilled that the stork
brought you a baby sister, air mail? Would you
like to see her?"
Little Boy: "Not really. But after that nine-
month flight, I'd sure like to see that stork!"

Janet Lanese

A three-year-old "big" sister constantly supervised Mother changing
the newborn. After one rushed session, completed without
the typical sprinkling of cornstarch, the child corrected Mom: "Wait!
You forgot to salt him!"

Anonymous

We were born ten minutes apart, Adrian first. She always said she was the real baby, and I was a kind of backup.

Adair Lara

I don't believe that the accident of birth makes people sisters or brothers. It makes them siblings, gives them mutuality of parentage. Sisterhood and brotherhood is a condition people have to work at.

Maya Angelou

Little girls are cute and small only to adults. To one another they are not cute. They are all life-sized.

Margaret Atwood

Though she left our family when she was only nine and I was ten,
the happiest memories of my childhood were those magical days
spent with my foster sister Barbara.

Janet Lanese

"What's your new sister's name?" a visitor asked the little boy.
"How would I know?" he answered. "I can't understand a word she says."

Anonymous

I love my little sister, but I refuse to take a bath with her.
She makes the bath water too dirty!

April, age five

A baby sister is nicer than a goat. You'll get used to her.

Lynne Alpern and Ester Blumenfeld

WHEN ANNIE WAS ADOPTED

When Annie was adopted,
Her brand new brother smiled;
He thought they were so lucky
To have a brand-new child.
He gave her tiny tickles,
Some kisses and a hug;
He tucked her in her basket
And wrapped her nice and snug;
And just before she fell asleep,
She looked at him and smiled
As though she knew already
She was their brand-new child.

Mary Ann Hoberman

When my sister Claudia was born, in 1947, the whole family constellation shifted. Suddenly there was the "baby" . . . suddenly there was a baby nurse who wouldn't let me touch the baby because I had caught ringworm from my best friend's cat.

Erica Jong

My sister Sarah is ten minutes younger than I am, making me the older sister, something I lorded over her for years. Until we were about nine, it seemed pretty logical to me that when I died, Sarah would automatically die ten minutes after me.

Lucy Grealy

Sign on the door of twin girls' nursery: Bawl Room.

Anonymous

I liked my sister a whole lot better when she was a baby.
All Mom had to do to keep her quiet was to change her diapers
and put a bottle in her mouth.

Jeffrey, age seven

When mother boasts cheerfully, "Johnny is just crazy about his new little sister.
You love her, don't you, dear?" Johnny hasn't much choice but to lie like
a gentleman . . . and then he begins to worry that something terrible may
happen to little sister. She might get eaten by a stray tiger or fall into a tub of
scalding water. It doesn't often occur to that grown-up to wonder why tigers
and tubs of scalding water are all of a sudden wandering around the house
waiting for an unwary moment.

Leotine Young

10 REASONS WHY EVERYONE SHOULD
HAVE A SISTER!

1. The common thread of family memories.
2. A friendly voice as close as the nearest phone.
3. The person who understands you the best.
4. Someone to share your joys and sorrows.
5. The one woman you can always count on.
6. The fun times of family get-togethers.
7. The one who loves you despite your faults.
8. Your best friend and confidante.
9. The comfort of never feeling alone.
10. The joy of growing older together.

Janet Lanese

Never envy an only child!
Not to feel the bond of close siblings
is to feel loneliness.

Janet Lanese

The question that's probably uppermost in the child's mind is:
Why do my parents want to have a baby? Don't they love me?
And if they love me, why do they need another one? Aren't I enough?
Imagine for a minute yourself in a similar situation.
Your husband comes home and says, "Honey, I love you so much,
I've decided to get another wife so I can have two." How would you feel?

Lawrence Butler

Friendship

and

Rivalry

The quickness with which all the "stuff" from childhood can
reduce adult siblings to kids again underscores the strong
and complex connections between brothers and sisters. It doesn't seem
to matter how much time has elapsed or how far we've traveled.
Our brothers and sisters bring us face to face with our former selves
and remind us how intricately bound up we are
by each other's lives.

Jane Mersky Leder

HOW TO TORTURE YOUR SISTER

- WANDER into the room when she calls a friend on the telephone. Pick up a book and sit down on the couch. Pretend to read, then mimic her as she begins her telephone conversation.

  Hi, how are you? *Hi, how are you?* Wha'd you do today? *Wha'd you do today?* What? Wait a minute, my sister's driving me crazy. Would you cut it out? *Would you cut it out?* You dirty creep. *You dirty creep.* Stop repeating me! *Stop repeating me!* I said STOP! *I said STOP!* STOP IT!! *STOP IT!!*

  Put down book and run.

- SHE is eating peanuts. Whisper in her ear, "You can turn into an elephant if you eat too many peanuts. I read it in the *World Book.*"
- FOLLOW her everywhere.
- IMITATE her best friend talking. Say that her best friend is fat.
- TALK to your mother while your sister is listening: "Do you remember Christmas when I was three years old and you gave me that stuffed animal? That was so much fun." Turn to your sister: "You weren't alive."

Delia Ephron

There can be no situation in life in which the conversation of my dear sister
will not administer some comfort to me.

Lady Mary Wortley Montague

Love lets the past die. It moves people to a new beginning without settling
the past. Love prefers to tuck the loose ends of past rights and
wrongs in the bosom of forgiveness—and pushes us into a new start.

Lewis B. Smedes

The best time I had with my big sister was the day I helped her pack to
go to college. Now her room is all mine!

Sandy, age ten

An older sister helps one remain half child, half woman.

Anonymous

Most of your sister's secrets are either not worth keeping or too good to keep.

Janet Lanese

My teacher told us the average family consists of 4.1 people.
I wonder if my little sister realizes she's the .1?

Kevin, age eleven

Elder sisters never can do younger ones justice!

Charlotte Bernikow

One is taught by experience to put a premium on those few people
who can appreciate you for what you are.

Gail Godwin

The same stars . . . the same moon looks down upon your brothers and sisters.

Sojourner Truth

Sisters are the easiest people in the world to forgive. Except when
they're the hardest. It's a question of balance.

Jeanne Marie Laskas

Sisters define their rivalry in terms of competition for the gold cup of
parental love. It is never perceived as a cup that runneth over,
rather a finite vessel from which the more one sister drinks,
the less is left for the others.

Elizabeth Fishel

10 THINGS YOU SHOULD NEVER
TELL YOUR SISTER

1. When she was seven, you sold her to a neighbor kid for a quarter.
2. Mom always loved you best.
3. You hate the way she dresses.
4. Dad just lent you $5,000 for a new car.
5. You think her kids are spoiled.
6. People always ask, "Which one of you is the youngest?"
7. She was adopted.
8. You always wanted to be an only child.
9. Your boyfriend thinks she's far less attractive than you.
10. She's just like Mom.

Linda Sunshine

As young children, my sisters and I were close. I enjoyed being the oldest, showing them around, protecting them. When a bully who sat across from Susan at the schoolroom table kicked her legs black and blue, I beat him up in the playground.

Patrick Ireland

Those who tease you, love you.

Jewish proverb

"You and your sister are twins. Right?"
"Well, we were until we were forty. Now she's five years younger than I am."

Janet Lanese

I'm not afraid to trust my sisters—not I.

Angelina Grimké

There is space within sisterhood for likeness and difference, for the
subtle differences that challenge and delight; there is space
for disappointment and surprise.

Christine Downing

You don't pick a sister, she is given to you randomly. Your relationship with her
may not be close in the beginning. However, in the end, it's up to you to figure
out how your sister can become your best friend.

Bernadette Szafranski

A woman should always stand by a woman.

Euripides

To most people, my sister and I didn't seem to have much in common,
but I knew . . . that we were remarkably alike.

Kathleen Norris

Sometimes I must drive her crazy. But she loves me anyway and never lets on.
She continues to guard my heart and nurture my soul.
My sister is a true blessing in my life.

Betty Pearl Hooper

More than Santa Claus, your sister knows when you've been bad or good.

Linda Sunshine

I like my sister a whole lot better for having a few faults
that I can talk about.

Stephanie, age seventeen

Only a sister can compare the sleek body that now exists with the chubby
body hidden underneath. Only a sister knows about former pimples,
failing math, and underwear under the bed.

Laura Tracy

No woman ever had a sister she didn't dislike at one time or another.

Janet Lanese

When there's a sibling
There's a quibbling.

Selma Raskin

Sibling rivalry is not an evil born of parental failure. It is a fact of life.

Seymour V. Reit

Approval from a sister weighs much heavier than from a friend, and your
sister's disapproval, like no one else's, can crush you
and fill you with doubt.

Diane Werts

When you were kids, she made you nuts. Much later, you discover why you hurt each other but love each other even more.

Patricia Volk

Why is it so hard to act like an adult around your sister? Where your sister is concerned, everything you do seems to be equal parts habit, compulsion, and voodoo forces beyond your control.

Lesley Dormen

MY PET SISTER

There once was an ad in a
paper I read, "Bring your pets to the flea
market," it said. "If you do not want them,
then bring them to us, And we'll find them new
homes, and You won't have to fuss." So I took my sister to the
flea market there. I showed them her pretty
blue eyes and brown hair. They said, "Are you serious?
She's not a PET!" And I said right back to
them, "You wanna bet?"

Jamie Klenetsky, Children's Digest

Of all the sisters in my family, I like me best!

Emily, age six

Nothing ruins a family reunion more than seeing an older sister who has managed to stay younger-looking than you and marry into money at the same time.

Jill Blount

Most sisters love to hear their sister laugh, but not necessarily when they break a heel on the dance floor.

Anonymous

Rivalry is better than envy.

Mongo proverb

MY SISTER, MY FRIEND

My sister's love is very special,
    one I'll treasure through the years.
We've played and laughed together
    and ofttimes shed many tears.
But through life's maze of problems,
    God placed a bond of love within
To unite our hearts in wisdom
    changing sisters into friends.

Judy Meggers

There is no one as easy and fun to tease as a sister—and who else
can be trusted to be so forgiving?

Laurie Harper

HOW TO BE AN OLDER BROTHER

You and your sister are in a restaurant. The waiter has not come to your table yet. He's taking orders at the table next to yours. Whisper: "Hey, that waiter's pretty cute, don't you think? Not bad, not bad at all. Look at that bod." Raise your voice. "Really, it's no trouble. Hey, waiter, waiter, my sister wants to meet you. Take it easy, it's okay, the waiter doesn't mind. He thinks you're cute, too. Don't you?"

Your sister had a date last night:
Wink at her. "Wearing a turtleneck, I see. Mom, have you ever noticed that every time she goes out with that guy, she wears a turtleneck the next day?"

Your sister is in the living room, talking to a boy. She introduces you. "Mark? This is Mark! Well, well, well. Excuse me, Mark, is that a pimple or did you cut yourself shaving?"

Delia Ephron

I was a goody-goody; she was more defiant . . . but despite our differences and petty rivalries—and apart from a period in my senior year when we grew estranged—we were always the best of friends.

Kathie Lee Gifford

Your worst critic is a younger sister who sees your finished work and never lets you forget that she could have done it better.

Janet Lanese

It takes two to make a quarrel, but only one to end it.

Spanish proverb

It's amazing how even the most difficult sister can be agreeable, if one keeps her mouth shut.

Janet Lanese

There was a time when my older sisters and their friends were just starting to kiss boys. They needed somebody to practice on. I'd sprint home from school, go in the bathroom, and they'd put me on the bathroom sink, and my sister's two friends would take turns kissing me. They taught me how to French kiss when I was eight years old.

The first time, I almost suffocated.

Tom Cruise

Last night I was good and helped my sister. I sat down on her bed and helped her cry.

Jennifer, age seven

I think if there's no sibling rivalry in a family, there's a lot of denial going on, because you can't help but rub against each other when you're forming who you are.

Joanna Kerns

If you don't understand how a woman could both love her sister dearly and want to wring her neck at the same time, then you were probably an only child.

Linda Sunshine

Sisterhood conjures up a welter of complex emotions. On a bad day, you envision your sister as the offspring of Genghis Khan and Mother Teresa. Or Cindy Crawford and the traitor Aldrich Ames. In the sister state, the emotional thermometer ricochets between love and hate. Who else can make you so angry? Who else can be so compassionate?

Brenda Hunter and Holly L. Larson

Sisters are for fighting with in the daytime and for loving in the nighttime. Especially when you say your prayers.

Sandy, age seven

When you are an adult, it is almost impossible to be a real friend to your sister
on any other terms except on the terms of equality.

Janet Lanese

Eventually, we will learn that the loss of indivisible love is another of
our necessary losses, that loving extends beyond the mother-daughter
child pair, that most of the love we receive in this world is love we
will have to share—and that sharing begins at home,
with our sibling rivals.

Judith Viorst

Mirror,
Mirror,
on the Wall

Brothers and sisters are as close as hands and feet.

Vietnamese proverb

Sisters examine each other so they can have a map for how they should behave.

Michael D. Kahn

Even the conjugal tie is beneath the fraternal. Children of the same family, the same blood, with the same associations and habits, have some enjoyment in their power, which no subsequent connections can supply.

Jane Austen

My twin sister and I share everything. Everything, that is, except
boyfriends and toothbrushes.

Michelle, age seventeen

My sister and I look different, act different, and have
different interests, but the important thing is
that we are the same inside.

Trish, age thirteen

Hallie and I . . . were all there was. The image in the mirror proves you are still here. We had exactly one sister apiece. We grew up knowing the simple arithmetic of scarcity. As a sister is more precious than an eye.

Barbara Kingsolver

Sisterly love is, of all sentiments, the most abstract.

Ugo Betti

One of the best things about being an adult is the realization that you can share with your sister and still have plenty for yourself.

Betsy Cohen

When someone prizes us just as we are, he or she confirms our existence.

Eugene Kennedy

A woman's best support is a dear sister.

Helen Stewart

It's hard as kids to know what's causing you to feel and react the way you do,
but as adults we worked through a lot of that stuff.
Now we're each other's best supporters.
No one knows her better than I know her, and vice versa.

Joanna Kerns

Even children of the same mother look different.

Korean proverb

Both within the family and without, our sisters hold up our images
of who we are and of who we dare to become.

Elizabeth Fishel

A sister can be seen as someone who is both ourselves
and very much not ourselves—
a special kind of double.

Toni A. H. McNaron

Family faces are magic mirrors. Looking at people who belong to us,
we see the past, present, and future.

Gail Lumet Buckley

Together we look like our mother. Her same eyes, her same mouth,

open in surprise to see, at last, her long-cherished wish.

Amy Tan

Lives of ancestors remind us,

we give photos to our kin,

and departing leave us behind

relatives who point and grin.

Anonymous

If sisters disagree, the bystander takes advantage.

Chinese proverb

Your sister is the only creature on earth who shares your heritage, history,

environment, DNA, bone structure, and contempt for stupid Aunt Gertie.

Linda Sunshine

A loyal sister is worth a thousand friends.

Marian Eigerman

We heard a song, we heard it in harmony.

Maxene Andrews, of the Andrews Sisters

We know one another's faults, virtues, catastrophes, mortifications,
triumphs, rivalries, and desires, and how long we hang
by our hands to a bar. We have been bonded together
under pack codes and tribal laws.

Rose Macaulay

As different as my sister and I are, I need only to look in the mirror and I
see her eyes, her mouth, her expression; then I remember all
that we have in common.

Laurie Harper

Miserable people cannot afford to dislike each other. Cruel blows of fate call for extreme kindness in the family circle.

Dodie Smith

The older daughter is married off by her parents, the younger daughter by her sister.

Russian proverb

THE OLDEST SISTER, AKA "THE NANNY"

There were advantages being the older sister, like a later curfew, and no hand-me-downs. But you were also expected to be a role model for your younger siblings. Do these parental remarks sound familiar?

"You have to realize that with privileges of the eldest come responsibilities."

"Babysitting your little sister prepares you for motherhood."

"What do you mean you got a B in math? Grades like that won't get you into Stanford!"

"Watch your mouth! You know how your sisters mimic you."

"How can you say your sister is your rival? She's your pal."

"You've got to learn to share. So what if your sister took your new CD player to school?"

"Your sister teases you because she wants your attention."

"So the baby bit your ear. Accidents do happen, you know."

Janet Lanese

THE MIDDLE SISTER, AKA "SECONDHAND ROSE"

As the sandwich kid whose identity often gets lost in the shuffle, did your mother ever use these lines on you?

"Isn't your big sister generous to give you her beautiful clothes to wear?"

"How lucky you are; it's a designer label."

"What do you mean you hate purple and yellow polka dots?"

"Of course it's still in style."

"Except for minor fading, you can hardly tell it's been worn."

"It'll be real comfortable now that it's broken in."

"It looks much nicer on you than it ever did on your sister."

"Stop complaining. You'll grow into it in a few months."

"Nobody is going to see that small patch under your armpit."

"Who will remember something your sister wore two years ago?"

Janet Lanese

THE YOUNGEST SISTER, AKA "THE BABY"

Because your parents were already worn out raising the others, you probably had "laid-back" parental guidance. You were a free spirit who rarely had to take responsibility for anything. However, there were a few drawbacks to being the youngest.

"No more stints as a Brownie troop leader. Can't you join an after-school activity that doesn't require my participation?"

"No new bike. You know your sister needs braces. All your old one needs is a new pedal."

"Funny, your other two sisters never had any trouble with that teacher."

"Do you act up just to be the center of attention, or should we have the doctor put you on Ritalin?"

"So your jeans are a little soiled. They're fine for another day."

"Stop sleeping on the living room floor. You should know it's past bedtime when the TV test pattern comes on."

"So what if your older sister has $95 Nikes? She's on the
school tennis team. For someone who isn't into sports, a
cheap pair from the thrift store is good enough."

"Over three hundred dollars to have your stomach pumped! I
warned you about eating all that junk food."

"Sorry I missed parents' night, but you know your sister was
the star of her school play."

Janet Lanese

No one knows
better than a sister
how we grew up, and
who our friends,
teachers, and
favorite toys were.
No one knows
better than she.

Dale V. Atkins

We shared Parents. Home. Pets. Celebrations. Catastrophes. Secrets. And the threads of our experience became so interwoven that we are linked. I can never be utterly lonely knowing you share the planet.

Pam Brown

The family is like a book,

    The children are the leaves,

The parents are the covers

    That protective beauty gives.

At first pages of the book

    Are blank and purely fair,

But time soon writes its memories

    And paints its pictures there.

Love is the little golden clasp

    That bindeth up the trust,

Oh, break it not, lest all the leaves

    Shall scatter and be lost.

Anonymous

It's a sure bet that any small girl who can laugh
after she just broke her mother's favorite vase has already thought
of a younger sister to blame it on.

Janet Lanese

As siblings, we were inextricably bound, even though our connections
were loose and frayed.

. . . And each time we met, we discovered to our surprise and dismay
how quickly the intensity of childhood feelings reappeared. . . . No matter how
old we got or how often we tried to show another face,
reality was filtered through yesterday's memories.

Jane Mersky Leder

You leave home to seek your fortune; and when you get it, you go home
and share it with your family.

Melba Moore

In one study of siblings over sixty, 83 percent said they were close or extremely
close to their siblings. Both men and women frequently name sisters
as the one they are more attached to—sisters, it seems, work hardest
at keeping the family together.

Patricia Nachman

I've found that once in a while sisters come in handy. Especially when only four players show up for your basketball team.

Daniel, age ten

It is true that I was born in Iowa, but I can't speak for my twin sister.

Abigail Van Buren

More and more I realize that everybody, regardless of age, needs to be hugged and comforted in a brotherly or sisterly way now and then. Preferably now.

Jane Howard

In families children tend to take stock roles, as if there were hats hung up
in some secret place, visible only to the children. Each succeeding child
selects a hat and takes on that role, the good child, the black sheep,
the clown, and so forth.

Ellen Galinsky

Other things may change us, but we start and end with the family.

Anthony Brandt

Family Life! The United Nations is child's play compared to the tugs and splits
and need to understand and forgive in any family.

May Sarton

If your sister is in a tearing hurry to go out and cannot catch your eye,
she's wearing your best sweater.

Pam Brown

On being asked which of his two sisters he liked best, the little boy responded,
"When I am with one, I like the other."

Anonymous

Always keep the other person's well-being in mind when you feel an attack of
soul-purging truth coming on.

Betty White

The best advice I can give to all girls over thirteen is that if you share a room
with your little sister, never keep a diary!

Monica, age sixteen

Writing this, I realize how sweet and slippery is this word "sister"—big enough
to stretch beyond biology and across time; enough to embrace me and Rene,
me and Betty, my two daughters, and the sisterhoods in between.

Letty Cottin Pogrebin

"Is Kim your sister?"

"Yes."

"And who comes after her?"

"You and two other guys."

Anonymous

Are big sisters always bossy? Do little ones always feel a lot of envy?
Someday, possibly, someone will put the personalities of millions of sisters
into a computer—and come out with somewhat scientific answers
to such questions.

Doris Faber

We flatter those we scarcely know,
We please the fleeting guest,
And deal full many a thoughtless blow
To those who love us best.

Ella Wheeler Wilcox

Nepotism is only kin deep.

Anonymous

Things hold. Lines connect in ways that last and last, and lives become
generations made out of pictures and words just kept.

Lucille Clifton

Blood's thicker than water, and when one's in trouble,
best to seek out a relative's open arms.

Euripides

Stacey, age eight, was advising her little sister that she would avoid

a lot of tears if she would refuse to spell her name.

"The minute you spell your name, you've had it!"

she said. "After that, the words

get harder and harder."

Anonymous

The great gift of family life is to be intimately acquainted

with people you might never even introduce

yourself to had life not

done it for you.

Kendall Hailey

We are not primarily put on this earth

to see through one another, but

to see one another through.

Peter De Vries

When my sister was small, my friends kept complaining
about her always hanging around. Now that she's sixteen,
they beg her to hang around.

Ted, age seventeen

Loneliness is the most terrible poverty.

Mother Teresa

Alone we can do so little; together we can do so much.

Helen Keller

We acquire friends and we make enemies, but our
sisters come with the territory.

Evelyn Loeb

There isn't much that I can do,
But I can share my flowers with you,
And I can share my books with you,
And sometimes share your burdens too,
As on our way we go.

Maude V. Preston

After the verb "to love," "to help" is the most beautiful verb in the world.

Bertha Von Sultner

Did you know that according to statistics, one out of every four people in the
United States is unbalanced? There is no need to be concerned
unless you have three sisters who
seem perfectly normal.

Anonymous

Ten-year-old Bobby was given the assignment to write an essay in
as few words as possible on two of life's greatest problems.
He wrote "twin sisters."

Anonymous

There is something so physical about sisterhood, some
body-memory too deep for words.

Kennedy Fraser

The best definition I ever heard of a family came from a nine-year-old
who gave the question a great deal of concentrated thought as she lay
in the bathtub and finally burst out with "I don't know exactly what a family is,
but I know one thing. Your friends can go off and say
they don't want to be your friend anymore, but people just can't go off
and say they don't want to be your family anymore."

Ann P. Eliasberg,
The New York Times Magazine

The

Sister's

Song

To have a loving relationship with a sister is not simply to have a buddy or confidante—it is to have a soul mate for life.

Victoria Secunda

There is so much left to be discovered about sisters, about how to bond late if one didn't bond early, about how to undo, or make gold out of what has been lost . . . or how to redistribute the gold and the frogs.

Erika Duncan

Nothing could ever come between us.

Jacqueline Kennedy Onassis, about her sister Lee

I love Eva and she loves me; and if anything happened to
me, she would die; and if anything happened
to her, I would die.

Zsa Zsa Gabor

MY SISTER

My sister is just a sister,

Not a basketball star.

She never runs away from me,

She never goes very far.

I wonder what she has to say,

If only it would be clear.

Maybe she wants to tell me

That a tornado is near.

Maybe she wants to tell me

What she has been through.

Maybe she wants to tell me—I love you.

Karli Anderson, Children's Playmate

There is no blessing like a faithful sister. Someone you can always count on to count on you. A best friend who knows all about you and loves you anyway.

Janet Lanese

Birth order also has a strong bearing on how you relate to your sister. Each slot in the family—oldest, middle, youngest—has distinct advantages and disadvantages. Few older sisters would trade their driver's license for a hand-me-down bike, and most younger sisters wouldn't trade the parental attention they get for a later curfew.

Diane Werts

The comfort of knowing that our bonds will survive despite our differences and that our connection provides each of us with a more accurate picture of ourselves enhances our chances of finding inner peace and satisfaction as we age together.

Jane Mersky Leder

Research shows that friendship between sisters ebbs and flows across the life cycle. Sisters are most often close as children, more distant as young adults, but close again as they mature and move into midlife and beyond.

Toni A. H. McNaron

I get so mad at my little sister that I wish she'd disappear. But then I start thinking, if that happened, who would I pick on?

Timothy, age eight

It is only the women whose eyes have been washed clear with tears who get broad vision that makes them little sisters to all the world.

Dorothy Dix

The continual sharing, the can't-wait-to-tell-my-sister is part of the bonding between sisters. It's a relationship that is not to be taken lightly.

Robert Strand

At sixty, it is a blessing to have a sister who is a little older. Let's face it, not all women our age are healthy and happy. Ann and I boost each other's self-esteem by sharing our own positive ideas and attitudes.

Sarah Stark

Sisters can be responsible for so many things: making you laugh, making you mad, stealing your first boyfriend, giving you your first niece. Part of you always putting back in a desire to be your own person, the rest of you needing to be close and nurturing the exclusive sense of security.

Jane Dowdeswell

Lord help the mister
Who comes between me and my sister,
and Lord help the sister
Who comes between me and my man!

"Sisters," by Irving Berlin

MY SISTER

My sister can do almost everything better than me.

At gymnastics, she can do a back flip—on the balance beam! (Coach says my cartwheels are getting much better.)

At school, my sister always colors inside the lines. (My teacher says my coloring is very "interesting.")

And when it's time for supper, my sister asks Mom, "May I set the table for you?"

Mom says, "Look at your sister. Isn't she a good helper?"

At home, my sister always hangs up her clothes and makes her bed. (I don't.)

And when it's time for supper, "Isn't she a good helper?"

My sister can do almost everything better than me—except whistle. She tries and she tries and she tries. But she can't whistle—not even one little note.

But I CAN!

So I whistle all the time. I whistle on the way to gymnastics. I whistle while my sister hangs up clothes and makes her bed. And I whistle while my sister sets the table.

Mom says, "Listen to your sister. Doesn't she whistle well?" (I just love my mom!)

My sister can do almost everything better than me.
But she can't whistle like me.

And I like it that way!

Jo Carol Herbert, Humpty Dumpty's Magazine

What's the simplest way to entertain your sister?
Just sit down and listen to her!

Janet Lanese

The relationship between two siblings is perhaps more like a cactus than an oak, for it requires less watering than other friendships in order to survive.

Susan Scarf Merrell

My sister is a bowl of golden water which brims but never overflows.

Virginia Woolf

Bless you, my darling, and remember you are always in the heart—oh tucked so close there is no chance of escape—of your sister.

Katherine Mansfield

Sisterly love is that nonsensical emotion that makes
you think almost as much of a sibling
as you do yourself.

Janet Lanese

What is a loving sister?
A single soul dwelling in two bodies.

Anonymous

Although many women look upon their sisters as best
friends, they are so much more than a pal or confidante
to each other. Who else knows every minute,
intimate detail of each other's personality
and idiosyncrasies? Secrets not dared shared
with Mother? Sisterhood is
a powerful bond.

Janet Lanese

There is only one substitute for the endearments of a sister, and that is
the endearments of some other fellow's sister.

P. J. O'Rourke

I don't know if I could live without her. My eyes flood writing this.
Picturing life without my sister is not possible. . . . I love her
as much as I love me. *Ma soeur, c'est moi.*

Patricia Volk

MY SISTER

My Sister, her high-pitched voice. The way she can catch almost anyone's attention. The way her mouth curls when she smiles. The way she can charm all the lower-grade teachers.

My Sister, the way she dresses herself in the morning. The way she knows how to get her way. The way she tries to do her hair. The way she can do anything she wants, and not look the other way at all.

My Sister, the way she can turn the world on with her smile. She can turn a nothing day and suddenly make it all seem worthwhile. And that's why I and everyone who knows her loves her.

Michael Robinson, age twelve

A "silent" sisterhood has always existed among women bound together
in networks of friendship, love, and mutual support.
But today the word "sisterhood" is not so silent and has much
broader significance. It denotes a feeling of pride among
women, as they now are helping one another
to realize their potential
as human beings.

Helene Arnstein

I have always been a great believer in birth order. I will chat with someone
for fifteen minutes and suddenly lunge at the "You're an oldest child,
aren't you?" That means something specific to me, about facing
the world and facing yourself. My husband is also the
eldest child, and the slogan one of his brothers coined for it
is instructive: either pope or president. Not in words
but in sentiment, my siblings felt the same about me.
A substantial part of my character arises from such expectations.

Anna Quindlen

Sisters are always drying their hair.
Locked in rooms, alone,
They pose at the mirror, shoulders bare,
Trying this way and that their hair,
Or fly importunate down the stair
To answer the telephone.

Phyllis McGinley

Kristen and Kathy are my youngest sisters. Although we have different fathers,
I don't think of them as half-sisters at all. They are complete sisters in
all senses of the word, unstinting in their teasing and devotion. And if
they were not my sisters, I'd want to be their friend.

Brett Butler

My oldest sister, Alice Lynn Foran, is the rock, the one you can call
at three in the morning, and she'll always be
ready to help in any way.

Reba McEntire

Sisterhood is to friendship what an arranged marriage is to romance. You are
thrown together for life, no questions asked (until later), no chance
of escape. And if you're lucky, you find love
despite the confinement.

Lisa Grunwald

Have you ever noticed that your sister's gripes are always a lot
more interesting if you have a few of your own?

Janet Lanese

Our pattern of sisterhood makes an ongoing spiral, and within that spiral
are our families, our communities, the earth, stars, all time. The
spiral resembles two women carrying water through
a battlefield in a rain of arrows. It resembles a long snake of relatives
who walk through history, from the eastern hills of time immemorial,
the light balances the dark. Wildness walks next
to her steady sister. They make it to the other side together.

Joy Harjo

Sisters

for

Life

HOW DO I FEEL ABOUT MY SISTERS?

They love me; they know me and they still love me.

I'd love to be skinny for Kathy.

I'd love to be more quiet like Deed.

I'd love to be able to handle my home like Janet.

They are my best friends.

They are me.

Peggy Lennon

My sister and I call each other frequently; we're keenly aware of the process of each other's lives, the ups and downs of marriage and work, family and health, the yearly vacations and Christmas. "What's happening?" my sister says when I pick up the phone. On my desk, I have papers to grade, the first page of a story I'm trying to write. I hear her children arguing in the background, then doors slamming, the intimate noises of family life. Yet for the moment, I know she's shut them out, focused totally on me. I feel her waiting, her breath drawing me closer.

I sit back in my chair, prop my feet up on the stool. "You just won't believe this," I begin. And I feel the tug of our secret life.

Patricia Foster

These are the memories we laugh about sitting on the front porch.
The day is hot and sticky. We have gathered as we often did
in those pink rooms to tell our stories—to share our
surprise at the women we have become—to talk
about the way we are now. All of us know
the joy of sustained sisterly bonding—
that is the legacy Rosa Bell,
our mother, gave us.
This is the legacy we will pass on.

bell hooks

I have always loved my sister's voice. It is clear and light, a voice
without seasons, like bells over a green city or snowfall
on the roots of orchids. Her voice is a
greening thing, an enemy
of storm and dark
and winter.

Tom Wing in Pat Conroy's The Prince of Tides

Having a sister means having one of the most beautiful and unique of human relationships.

Robert Strand

It's a great comfort to have an artistic sister.

Louisa May Alcott

Often in old age, they become each other's chosen and most happy companions. In addition to their shared memories of childhood and of their relationship to each other's children, they share memories of the same home, the same homemaking style, and the same small prejudices about housekeeping that carry the echoes of their mother's voice.

Margaret Mead

I cannot deny that now I am without your company I feel
not only that I am deprived of a very dear sister,
but I have lost half myself.

Beatrice D'Este, letter to Isabella

Bessie and I have been together since time began, or so it seems.
Bessie is my little sister, only she's not so little.
She is 100 years old, and I'm 103.
After so long, we are in some way
like one person.

Sarah L. ("Sadie") Delany

It occurs to me that one can never grow up with one's sister.

In some secret place we remain seven and eight.

And yet we are always family, tied by bonds so deep,

so invisible the soft blue noises of love

rush through our bodies, surprising me,

waking us as from sleep.

Patricia Foster

When his sister died in 1925, Will Rogers attended her funeral. Many

newspapers printed: Mrs. C. L. Lane, sister of the famous

comedian Will Rogers. "They are greatly misinformed.

It's the other way around.

I am the brother of Mrs. C. L. Lane, the friend of humanity.

And I want to tell you, all these people

who were there to pay tribute to her memory,

it was the proudest moment of my life that I was her brother."

Will Rogers

I think the need for sisters is innate.
Out of that need we look for a sister surrogate.
The most profound female friendships often emerge out
of women who were unsistered.

Sue Monk Kidd

Sisters are our peers, the voice of our times.

Elizabeth Fishel

Sisters are the sunshine of life.

Sue Stewart

You are my sister
and my beautiful lifelong friend.
You listen to my heartaches
and laugh with me
through every joy.
You know me better than anyone else.
You love me
even when I don't feel
that I deserve it.
You believe in me
when no one else
seems to.
You'll always be
my precious sister
and a special part of me.
I love you.

Laurel Goff

One's sister is a part of one's essential self, an eternal presence
of one's heart and soul and memory.

Susan Cahill

Sisters stand between one and life's cruel circumstances.

Nancy Milford

A ministering angel shall my sister be.

Shakespeare

You know full as well as I do the value of sisters' affections to each other;
there is nothing like it in this world.

Charlotte Brontë

Is solace anywhere
more comforting
than in the arms
of sisters?

Alice Walker

I'd notice the beautiful faces of my two sisters—their facial bones, their

very eyes. Mary was the beauty. She had blonde

hair and blue eyes, and even as a child,

long long legs.

Martha Graham

I have nothing against undertakers personally.

It's just that I wouldn't want one to bury my sister.

Jessica Mitford

A true sister is a soulmate who listens with her heart.

Anonymous

Help one another, is part of the religion of sisterhood.

Louisa May Alcott

We older women who know we aren't heroines can offer our
younger sister, at the very least, an honest report
of what we have learned and
how we have grown.

Elizabeth Janeway

Life has no blessing like a loving sister who understands you.

Janet Lanese

My sister taught me everything I really need to know, and she was
only in the sixth grade at the time.

Linda Sunshine

As you face the golden years, you discover
you can count on only three friends: an old dog,
old money, and a younger sister.

Janet Lanese

If you and your sister take time to do things one-on-one
away from the extended family, a new pattern of
dealing with each other—and a new
friendship—is free to emerge.

Kim Wright Wiley

I FOUND MY SISTER

Long ago, when I was four,
I had a second brother.
I told my mom, right there and then,
please don't bring home another.
"You got the order wrong," I said.
"Can't you just exchange him?"
My dreams about a sister
are wearing mighty thin.
Not 'til I was ten years old
did I finally get my wish.
By then, she was like a doll to me,

or a dog or a cat or a fish.
I dressed her up and changed her pants,
and took her for a walk.
She wasn't good for much at all.
She couldn't even talk.
But in the winter when it was cold,
I found that she was handy.
I'd put her in my bed at night.
As a heater, she was dandy.
When she was four, I left home
to go away to school.
The things we never shared as sisters
were gone, I thought. How cruel!
Time went by, so far apart.
She finished college and wed.
How can it be so many years
since she heated up my bed?
I didn't know how lucky we were
to have never shared the bad

When we met again as grownups,

good memories were all we had.

You'd think we'd feel like strangers.

Somehow that isn't true.

She looks like me, talks like Mom

and it's Dad's humor that shows through.

We have so much in common,

despite the years apart.

We missed the shared experiences,

but we bonded at the heart.

She's my alter ego now.

It's a psychic link, you know.

I dreamed up a sister when I was four,

but we needed time to grow.

So, if your dream's worth dreaming,

Don't give way to fears.

For me to find my sister,

Took only forty years.

Gini Sunnergren

Permissions Acknowledgments

p. 11

Reprinted with the permission of Atheneum Books for Young Readers, an imprint
of Simon & Schuster Children's Publishing Division, from *If I Were in Charge of the
World and Other Worries*, by Judith Viorst. Text copyright © 1981 Judith Viorst.

p. 15

From *Fathers, Mothers, Sisters, Brothers*, by Mary Ann Hoberman; illustrated by
Marilyn Hafner. Copyright © 1991 by Mary Ann Hoberman.
By permission of Little, Brown and Company.

p. 24

"How to Torture Your Sister," from *How to Eat Like a Child*, by Delia Ephron.
Illustrated by Edward Koren. Copyright © 1977, 1978 by Delia Ephron.
Illustrations Copyright © 1978 by Edward Koren. Used by permission
of Viking Penguin, a division of Penguin Putnam Inc.